THE ISLAND
MODEL

SELF RECODING

by Daisy Papp

ISBN -13: 978-1981924028

ISBN -10: 1981924027

TABLE OF CONTENTS

ABOUT THIS BOOK

Long before I visited Florida for the first time in 1992, my dream was to live on an island. Salt water, endless summers, sun-kissed skin; these were all attractive to me in my dream-place. Not knowing that I already lived on an island my entire life, metaphorically, I tried to find answers: where could I find beauty, inner peace, harmony, balance, plus friendly and sincere like-minded people? My extensive travels around the globe made me realize that there must be more to it, there must be a deeper root to be discovered. I tried to understand my life experience from many angles, and I wondered how it could be possible that visiting some of the most beautiful, exclusive, sometimes incredibly luxurious places did not add to my contentedness. Worse, I remember sitting in the Villa d'Este at Lake Como, a former 16th century royal residence, with tears running down my cheeks. It became apparent to me that it was not the outside world that would possibly bring me the inner balance and peace of mind, but all that I held within me: my thoughts, the words I speak to myself over and again, the pictures and short movies playing in my head. The more organized my inner world became, the more I grew able to observe the outer world from a relatively neutral point of view. What a joy! The more we know what we are doing within ourselves, the greater is our chance to live a life where our curiosity leads us to discover the treasures of existence with a very open mind. In the following pages, you can read about a simple, easy to apply, yet life-changing tool. I assure you it'll change your insights and outlook alike. Be ready for some unexpected "Ah-ha!" moments, and enjoy the freedom The Island Model brings to you, your loved ones, your life and theirs.

DEDICATION

I dedicate this book to my chosen hometown, the City of Marathon, in my beloved Florida Keys, and to all metaphorical Islanders who have supported me to further develop this model. By observing great, good, challenging, impossible, moody, provoking, understanding, loving, ignorant, arrogant, faithful, unfaithful, honest and dishonest behaviors, my curiosity has never ebbed away. Why people do what they do when they do it? My purpose with this publication is to raise awareness regarding differences, and commonalities, so that tolerance and acceptance can reach all – those who judge and those who are judged.

My enduring vision is to make this world a better place. One person at the time, starting with myself. One island at the time, including mine.

PREFACE

D o you ever wonder how many things you actually like, that you only *think* you like? Which of your preferences are really yours, and which are conditioned, culturally and traditionally expected, adapted, or simply just habits? Are your likes and dislikes still up-to-date? How many of your preferred activities, hobbies, and routines – yes, also your thinking habits and routines – are supporting you in your quest to live a content and balanced life?

Objective reality does exist; but not one human I know of can perceive it objectively. We all have filters through which we perceive our surroundings, and we all have our individual past. When you open your mind, when you reawaken your inborn curiosity, opportunities develop into possibilities. In the end, you may even become a habitual island-hopper. Read on and find out for yourself!

SELF RECODING

THE ISLAND MODEL

T he Island Model is an *invention/intervention* of German psychologist Vera F. Birkenbihl (1946-2011). As a pioneer of brain-friendly education and management training solutions, she was one of the most sought-after and highly acclaimed management trainers in German-speaking countries. Although the Island Model was not my idea originally, I have continued to further develop this powerful theory and tool over the years. Through my humble experience using the model with hundreds of clients over thousands of sessions conducted, I have witnessed an almost miraculous increase in mindfulness, emotional intelligence, and personal growth in the individuals with whom I've worked, and all of that within a very short amount of time. This incredible, easy-to-understand, and quite visual approach to how we humans create the world we live in is truly life-changing. My one-on-one clients, and seminar-, workshop-, and group session-attendees, who range from thirteen to eighty-three years of age, all gain a new perspective and insight that supports their personal growth, evolution, understanding of the world, and life itself. Tolerance becomes their new standard. The dynamics in all of their relationships shift to unexpected planes. Additionally, the quality of their relationship with themselves changes to a more respectful and loving one.

In everyday communication, things can go awry, especially when different personality types, cultures, and value systems meet and are mixed up – not to mention the impact the variety of linguistic styles and/or language barriers have on us humans.

One example of this could be when one talks *past* another, meaning that the content is not received and therefore feedback will be blurry and understanding becomes almost unfeasible. Possible consequences – besides the failed achievement of the goal of healthy communication – include a pejorative attitude in relation to the other person and/or avoidance of contact with the conversational partner.

However, *The Island Model* supports the improvement of overall communication, intra- and inter-communication alike, resulting in enhanced quality of all relations and relationships for the better.

The Island Model and its theory help bring some light into the dark at last. It is an aid to create more tolerance, acceptance, and understanding between us all: especially tolerance, acceptance, and understanding of *ourselves*.

THE METAPHOR AND HOW IT WORKS

I n this model, we imagine that every individual lives *in* their own island.

Not *on* an island. If we lived *on* an island, we could go ahead and leave that island at any given time. Trust me, I've tried to escape at times (more often than not, actually). One example I can mention offhand is when I was in the process of moving to Australia many years ago. Arriving in Queensland I truly, naively believed that I had left all my problems and challenges far behind on the European continent. Soon it became rather clear to me (within one week) that the challenges I faced *Down Under* were about the same as before.

The people in the scenarios had different initials, shoe sizes, citizenships, etc., but the dynamics and situations seemed to be copycats of what I believed myself to have left behind. Until I realized: "Oh, I took myself with me!" What an epiphany I had! I came to realize that there must be something *within me* that I carry with me wherever I go that eventually needs my attention (sooner rather than later) and should be addressed to support changes in my life for the better. There is a quote about this in *The Graveyard Book* by Neil Gaiman. "It's

DAISY PAPP

like the people who believe they'll be happy if they go and live somewhere else, but who learn it doesn't work that way. Wherever you go, you take yourself with you. If you see what I mean."

So let's imagine we are each living *in* an island and let's add that *in* this island is everything that we've already experienced in our lives. This island represents the world of each individual, shaped by his or her respective culture, traditions, personal habits, ideas, beliefs, opinions, etc. – everything that we consider "normal," "standard," or "the norm." Add to that all memories, experiences education, conditioning, expectations, fears, dreams, disappointments, failures, shame, blame, and resentment from the past – plus how we perceived, evaluated, and processed all of it – that made us who we are today; how we think and how we feel.

Contact between two people from different islands can be either good or bad, depending on our individual evaluation and the processing of the given situation. As I described in my book *The Formula for Finding True Love,* our bodies always follow our thoughts. And wherever we put our focus, our body will automatically create the matching feelings.

If, and/or when, the communication between two *islanders* is going well, we may consider ourselves lucky. The islands overlap, the communication seems easy and pleasant, the interlocutors see things in a similar way. We perceive our interaction as likeable, intelligent, and amicable, which usually creates the feeling that a good and exciting discussion and verbal exchange has come about.

However, if communication does *not* succeed as we've anticipated and we consider ourselves (and/or feel) unlucky, the consequence is *distance*, because the islands do not overlap. This distance is often a challenge to overcome because we have not learned (we were not conditioned to) *how* to respect that other people have other islands, with a different structure and subjective contents. Others love their islands just as much as we love ours! I'd say understandably so.

If there are big differences, whether culturally or due to contrasting habits or socialization and conditioning, we may find ourselves negligible, sometimes even indifferent, although our true values would whisper the contrary to us. Our conditioned default settings may come to fruition, causing us to use the learned, yet unflattering skill of talking past each other or take a condescending attitude towards the interlocutor.

It may also happen that we avoid contact with the other islander completely, which may not always be suitable, especially in professional life, family settings, neighborhoods, communities, etc.

BUILDING BRIDGES – BRIDGING THE GAP

T he question may arise: how can we possibly build bridges towards each other from island to island instead of burning them? We can learn more opportune communication skills once we accept that we actually all live in our own individual bubble, *in* our own island, in our own, small world.

If, and/or when, communication between two *islanders* threatens to fail, we should be able to build bridges to make up for the distance between two individuals and their two islands. Wouldn't you agree? We humans were apparently capable of flying to the moon! So it should be(come) possible to find creative ways to build bridges from one human to another.

Here is one helpful way to ground ourselves. Let's have a look from a different angle to gain a (very) unusual perspective. When we observe humans' physical shells – their bodies – there are clearly visible differences. One individual may have lots of hair, another one may be bald. Then there are mustaches, tattoos, makeup, one is taller than another, gender differences, amount of skin pigmentation, and weight, just to name few. When we zoom in and look inside a body at the organ level, we may discover that one person's heart (or liver, brain, stomach, lung, or kidney) is larger or appears healthier than another person's. If we zoom in a little further, we can see cells. At this level, our amazing immune system detects any organism that is not familiar – an intruder, so to speak – and our bodies reject any incompatibility, such as in a blood transfusion, bone marrow, or other organ donation. When we turn up the magnification to have an even closer look, we realize that our cells contain molecules, and molecules are made up of even smaller components called atoms. We are all made of atoms! Atoms are made up of particles called protons, electrons, and neutrons, and even scientists don't know of what those are composed. What we *do* know about particles is that they are connected all across the universe.

So consider what and/or whom we believe we are from smallest to largest: particles, atoms, molecules, cells, tissues, and organs. I am not a scientist, but I admit that I truly admire the depth of knowledge in their field(s) that has brought "*Namaste*" and "we are all the same" into a brand new context for me. On the atomic level, we are not differentiable or distinguishable. Now think about that for a second, if not for a minute or an hour! I think it will take me a lifetime to grasp.

ARE ISLANDS AND ISLANDERS CONDITIONED?

Here's yet another bit(e) of food for thought. Let me challenge you. Can you prove that if you were born in India to Indian parents, raised and conditioned to be a "good" Indian, you would not behave like an Indian based on those standards? Or can you prove that you would not behave like a royal to an extent, if you were born into a royal family that expected, conditioned, and domesticated you to live by their standards regarding royal behavioral patterns? Prove to me *how* you would not have believed what you believed growing up if you were born into a different religion/faith. For example, I am convinced that, if I had been born in China, I would not like to hug even those individuals closest to me, as it is not considered decent or proper to hug in China. I am a big hugger, but I would most likely not be the super hugger I am, had I been conditioned differently.

In one of my recent workshops, a lady verbalized her concerns regarding her son who is currently based overseas with the US forces. The son was advised to secure and supervise a square in the Middle East. All day long, the site appeared to be a quiet place. Children played, mothers walked, men conversed. Nothing unusual. But then, on a random Friday, the square turned into a busy public spot, and it got loud. For reasons that will become clear, policemen took off their belts. Within minutes, the square turned into a nightmare stage for summary execution. People streamed from all directions to observe as "convicted felons" were publicly punished and/or executed. Some thieves got their finger(s) or hand(s) cut off, liars lost their lips, others their ears. Noses were cut off of women who were (believed to be) unfaithful. I could go on and on describing the horrific methods of severe punishment displayed.

The young US soldier could not fathom how the children could witness such cruelty, watching the appointed, hated executioner carry out the judgments and then shift back to normalcy within minutes. They would just casually go back to play as if nothing happened! Let me be clear: I personally disfavor violence in all shapes and forms. But if I were born there as one of yon children, playing on those grounds, doing what all the others do, I would most likely do the same: play, witness, and then return to play again. Not because I would like it, but simply because it would be the norm in my culture. The standard, so to say. Natural to my peers and me. It would be exactly what I would have seen all my life, and what I'd have learned to accept it without scrutinizing or doubting. I'd probably even justify the acts and facts, maybe simply because my parents believed this to be the right thing to do, and so did their parents, their parents' parents, and so on. And if no one dared challenge whether it was right or not, neither would I. Again, this doesn't make the wrong right!

By the way, the reason the policemen take off their belts: the crowd becomes so excited that they want to see more and more executions, and the police use their belts to shoo away the people who are becoming almost high on the visual experience and want to see more cruelty.

Another example of conditioning: Some years ago I worked with a client from the United States who started professional relations with a European company. When they met for business lunches and dinners he worried that he might offend his overseas partners and colleagues due to different rules of etiquette. He remembered that I was born and raised in Europe, so he called me in a panic. He hoped I could advise and teach him standard European table manners. You may laugh at this and ask the legitimate question: "How do table manners even matter in business?" Well, let me inform you, he felt it was essential in order to succeed and prosper with this new opportunity.

So I had him visit me in my office, which was in Miami Beach back in those days. I packed all kinds of plates from home, including silverware, wineglasses, water glasses, napkins, dessert dishes, bread knives, etc., and set the table. I kindly invited him to sit at my desk, pretending we were at a gourmet restaurant waiting to be served. What caught my eye first and foremost was that he kept his left hand under the table, on his lap. When I grew up it was considered – in Germany – almost an insult to not have both hands on the table at all times. Think of the Island Model for a moment. All that we've experienced: conditioning, domestication, traditions, beliefs, habits, rituals, etc. I knew that he was neither born with the tendency nor the intention of insulting my cultural background, upbringing, or me personally. I tried to walk *over to* the imaginary metaphorical bridge and see what was *in* his island to find out why he kept his left hand under the table resting on his lap.

Raised in New Jersey, my client's family valued etiquette and strictly enforced the standard American table manners. My client was taught to eat with his right hand while keeping the left hand under the table at all times. To add to the confusion, when he was five or six years old (after the parents divorced), the little boy was introduced to his new stepfather, who happened to be a sophisticated French Canadian who grew up in Paris, France. The stepfather's standard was to keep both hands on the table while dining. The biological father, on the other hand (pardon the pub!), expected the young boy to keep his left hand under the table. Whenever my client was in the company of his father and mistakenly confused the rules, he got slapped on his hand! Please, imagine this for a moment: a little boy getting punished for having his left hand

under the table in the company of his stepfather, as well as by his dad for having both hands **on** the table.

Now, this may seem a stupid thing, and why would you even engage in reading any further? But let's go back to the Island Model again. Bio-dad enforces one hand on and one hand under the table. Step-dad enforces both hands on the table. Who is right? You may remember the illustration below from my book *The Formula for Finding True Love*. Let's assume you and I sit across from each other at a table and there is a piece of paper lying in the center. I draw the number six (6) on the piece of paper. But as you are sitting on the opposite side, what do you see? The number nine (9). Correct? So, who is right? We are both right. It is a question of perspective, and also a question of perception. I hope you agree that we both were right in the described scenario. We agree to disagree. (Haha – did I trick you?)

It is not about being right or wrong. Being right is not important, at least to me. (No one is smart enough to always be right, and no one is stupid enough to always be wrong.) My point here is to invite and inspire you to open your mind, go visit other islands, see that *you may be right while you're wrong at the same time*. Simple as that. More often than not, we can see the other person's viewpoint just by asking ourselves first. We only need to verbalize, "How come you see it this way?" to our conversational partner if absolutely necessary. When we really listen to understand, such an increase in peace can be reached with very little effort. Without building bridges, humanity could end up very isolated, very soon. As if we were not isolating ourselves already enough! Looking around, we can often observe groups of lonely people, playing on their smart devices in the middle of a crowd. I hope to see people connecting with each other again, sharing their ideas, thoughts, feelings, etc. without looking to judge, but rather to understand. Let's walk over these metaphorical bridges more often than not. Only then can we really decide if we like the content in others' islands. Otherwise we will consciously choose ignorance instead of wondering, asking questions, and observing what treasures might be found. Prejudice can dissolve, curiosity can increase, and connections may be built when we become bridge-builders.

By the way, do you know *why* the majority of the American population rests their left hand on their lap while eating? In the past, it was considered safer to eat with one hand and keep the other hand on the trigger of a gun! Yet people still do it all the time. Next time you go to a restaurant, look around and see for yourself. Outdated? Maybe so.

HAUNTED BY THE PAST – PROJECTIONS

U nless you live on a geographically remote island where you never encounter other humans, you most likely observe other islanders, and then projections sneak in subconsciously. For example, someone may look a little like a person we knew in the past, and suddenly we are just not in the present moment any longer but are wandering the paths of our internal past. Remember, the past doesn't exist! Did it happen? No question about it; what happened, happened. How we re-construct the past is on us. (Our brains reconstruct pictures, voices, sounds, feelings, and so forth. Our bodies respond to the reconstructions, and all feels real again.) Sometimes, others' behaviors remind us of other islanders that caused us hurt in our yesteryears. "Be careful!" I'd suggest. Observing objective reality is a quite limited task that we engage in daily. We can all identify a chair as a chair. What this particular chair *means* to us individually is very subjective.

For example, while I may have once fallen off a chair, you may have received a proposal from your loving partner while seated on a similar looking chair. So, our feelings towards the perceived chair, which is undoubtedly real, may be very different. Do you follow me here? Past hurts will haunt us in one way or another, and unresolved issues create more issues. We are all hurt to a degree. Some of us more, and luckily, some of us less.

Let me invite you to partake in a little experiment. I will give you a single word, and you have to take note of the first thing that comes into your mind. So, here's the word:

WATER.

Notice the first image, feeling, or sensation that comes to you.

Is the image in color or black and white? Do your taste buds respond to the word "water", or do you feel a physical sensation of longing for liquid? Is there a specific sensation you can observe in your body?

Whatever popped up first provides a great revelation as to what you hold within. If you have ever experienced a near drowning, your body may respond with reconstructed feelings of fear and images of threatening amounts of water surrounding you without a visible escape route. If you are a meteorologist, you may think of clouds first, or imagine measuring rain in inches, but if you are a figure skater preparing for the Winter Olympics, your mental, physical, or emotional response may vary, even though the element of water does not change. It is the meaning we give to our surroundings that changes the impact it has on us.

You might consider the instinctive reaction a firefighter, an oceanographer, a diver, a painter, a chef, or a swimmer would have. Or how about someone who grew up at the beach compared to someone who was raised in the desert? Depending on our subjective experiences, we individually relate to water (as an element) in different ways. When we realize that other islanders have varying relations to everything and anything, we can develop more tolerance, understanding, acceptance, compassion, and empathy.

WHERE IS YOUR FOCUS?

Focus on what you can control - Stop focusing on what you cannot control

D o you know how much energy you dedicate to various aspects of your life? In my workshops and seminars, I like to ask questions, sometimes at the beginning like a little quiz, or randomly inserted throughout. One of my favorite questions to ask is, "What do you worry about?" Some attendees giggle at my curiosity, some sigh. Most of the time the answers go directly to specific situations, people, circumstances. But that is not really what I am looking for. I interrupt that thread of thought by giving three categories in which the worries have to fit. Then I ask attendees to write down, as a percentage, how much they worry and in which category the worries belong. The end result must equal 100%. Here are the three categories:

What do you worry about?

1. Little things
2. Things you cannot change (i.e. the weather)
3. Things that will never happen

Allow me to give you an example for category three. Let us assume you are driving from point A to point B. You know that at your destination, B, it is quite a challenge to find a parking spot. Even before you depart point A, you sit in your car and worry about the parking. During your drive, you have all kinds of thoughts, remembering occasions where you were forced to park far, far away as there was an event in the area and police blocked most streets you were familiar with. You feel anxious as you get closer to your destination. You may even verbalize your opinion about other motorists on the road. Traffic is secondary at this moment as you are getting all wound up. You finally arrive and see... What is that, just in front of you? A free parking spot! All your worries were for nothing!

Remember to put all your worries into the categories listed above. At the end, they must add up to 100%. You will see that this self-assessment gives you a very different perspective. You may also see how much effort you could be saving. Sounds like an insurance ad, right?

I assume that you found out that most of your energy regarding worries goes into categories two and three. Let's go back to the Island Model again. You can now state that you have looked at your worries. How many people do you know who conduct a self-inventory regarding their concerns from time to time, or at all?

Then again, do you ever spare a thought for the worries other people may have? We all have worries, and that's ok. The question is how much we dwell on them. You could probably explain, if you were asked, why you worry about certain things. I respect you and your worries. I know that you have your reasons to feel the way you do. And if I were raised like you, believed what you believe, lived the days you lived the way you did, while thinking what you thought, I most likely would worry just like you do. This goes both ways though. I often hear how upsetting it is when people are told, "What? That's what you worry about? Shut up! That's stupid!" "Look at my problems! These are real concerns to worry about!" or otherwise. So one individual diminishes the other's worries but justifies their own? Wow! What a double standard!

I know a man who is constantly judging himself regarding his eye color. Because his mother had bright green eyes, she made him believe that his brown eyes were the reflection of his dark soul. (Forgive them, for they know not what they do...) Let me ask you: do you remember choosing your eye color? I bet you don't. Is it worth him wasting his time on something that he cannot change? (Well, there are contact lenses, I know. More on that later!)

When I was a little girl, I was told the tale that people with green eyes are more likely to be cheaters with emotionally ice-cold personalities than those with brown eyes. Others with blue eyes, they told me, would never be deeply in love, but enjoy kissing and are charming, and also would never lie. I am aware that likes and dislikes regarding eye colors do really exist, but is it really the amount of pigmentation that causes a person with blue eyes to be more likely to be faithful?

I am trying to ask questions so that you may challenge yourself, as well as others, and ask where at least some of these kinds of false beliefs originate. Of course, I have met cheaters with brown eyes, and charmers with brown eyes. Today I know for a fact that eye color is not an indicator, or external expression, of values and character traits. Nevertheless, many tales still abound and are believed regarding eye color. I knew this girl who lived in my neighborhood. Whenever she went out on a date she would wear colored contact lenses! When her dates were under 30 years of age, she wore green contacts, as she believed this age group preferred that color. Meanwhile, for dates over the age of 30, she went blue-eyed, to match her perception of *their* preference!

My ophthalmologist explained to me that blue eyes really are more sensitive to sun light. That's a scientific fact. Is that charming or not? I'll leave it up to you! Regardless, humans should be respected equally no matter what pigment count they have in their eyes. A faithful husband is a faithful husband. A lying neighbor is a liar. An abusive woman is an abuser. I could go on with this list. We cannot change the pigment count of ours or others' eyes. However, nowadays, I increasingly hear that it is a specific behavior that upsets people about another person – not the color of their eyes. They have come to recognize, at least, that it is not really the amount of pigmentation but rather behavioral styles that are disliked.

My purpose is not to convince you to change your beliefs and/or thinking. If you love brown eyes? So be it. What I sincerely wish is to inspire you to take inventory from time to time, to see which of your ideas, opinions, beliefs, etc. are still relevant, and what is outdated and possibly illogical.

WHAT CAN WE CHANGE? OURSELVES.

Personally, I believe that we do not have the right as humans to try to force others to change. I also believe that it is possible to inspire and live by example. We do not need to look far: when we observe children, it becomes rather clear that imitation is considerably more than simply copying. A mother walking with a stroller, spending most of her time on the phone, will have difficulty inspiring her child to look around and discover the world. It is also a challenge to raise a considerate future driver when the child is traveling with adults who drive recklessly and speed in school zones, for example. Children learn easily by observation, often without even paying too much attention. When a child grows up in a family where sarcasm is chronic, chances are that a future sarcastic pro is in the making. When a child grows up in an environment where meals are an important routine, where the food is cherished, and time spent at the dining table is used to share quality moments, chances are that a sound relationship with food and eating will be naturally established. Most standards, norms, and values are set very early on in life. When we accept this fact, it becomes easier to take on the role of an observer instead of becoming a judge. We can even learn to be more patient with ourselves.

Why do we do what we do? How often do we take inventory of our beliefs and standards? I suggest we take a closer look into our own individual islands. Let's find treasures, and let's also find those default settings that may not be suitable for living a content life. If we grew up in an environment where judgment was harsh and rude, we probably also remember how hurtful that experience was. What makes us think that when we judge now it is a pleasant experience for our fellow humans on neighboring islands? Judgments cannot bring us closer, as it most likely triggers defense mechanisms. How can we continue to justify racism or rudeness, sarcasm, bad mouthing, etc. simply because that's all we knew when we grew up? Change is unpreventable. Isn't it time to grow up now and take full responsibility for our actions, silent and loud alike? One could say: "Why me? Why should I change?", "Others should change, not me!", or "I'll change when he/she changes!" It is not about the other person. We can inspire others by leading by example.

JUDGMENTS ALWAYS FURTHER THE GAP

"If we could change ourselves, the tendencies in the world would also change. As a man changes his own nature, so does the attitude of the world change towards him... We need not wait to see what others do."

– Mahatma Gandhi

T he way I see it today, there is only one place for change, and that is within ourselves, in our own metaphorical island. I invite you to challenge your beliefs, habits, routines, actions, worries, etc., and ask yourself frequently if it is still worthwhile to keep them as they are, or better to let go of those that don't serve you any longer. According to a friend and great teacher of mine, Dr. Eric Dickhaus (neuroscientist and renowned researcher), the recipe for joint happiness is quite simple: "The secret to be happy with another person is to find the treasures they have within. Realize that you'll die before you find even a significant fraction of it and therefore never lose time looking at the defects. They are a distraction which will reduce the amount of treasures you will find or get."

I couldn't agree more. It may not always be easy to focus on the treasures to be found; nevertheless, it is well worth it. Go treasure hunting in your own island and the islands of others. Invite others to your island and go visit theirs. I hope I can inspire you to build bridges instead of burning them. Bridging the gaps is possible. The challenge I see us facing in our present day is that the temptation toward shallowness is greater than ever before. I also see masks falling off. So many humans seem to be on autopilot, doing things the way they have always been done without trying to get to the bottom of things, to the roots. On the other hand, you may realize that trying to change something in your partner could easily belong in one of the three "worries" categories – little things, things you cannot change, and things that will never happen, such as the changes you desire. We want to be loved for who we are, don't we? Our treasures want to be found, lived, loved, and appreciated. So do the treasures of other islanders.

I recently visited a restaurant where they invite great musicians to play – a different talent every night. There were some tables still available when I walked in. Unusually for me, I chose a high table with bar stools. At the next table sat a lady, probably in her late forties. She was dressed very casually, which is quite common in the Florida Keys. Her demeanor, nevertheless, struck me as gentle and kind. During a short break I turned towards her and asked: "Are you his biggest fan?" referring to the guitarist playing that night. "Yes, I am," she answered softly. This was no give-away; I wondered if she was his wife, girlfriend, sister, or someone else much closer to him than just a fan? On his way back to play, the musician saw us conversing, walked over towards us, and asked if there was a specific song we'd like him to play. My *King of Hearts* suggested "Little Wing" arranged by Stevie Ray Vaughn. And so he went on. What an ear-pleasing delight! I saw the lady's foot clearly moving to the beat, elegantly.

During yet another break, the guitarist came visit our tables again. All three of us introduced ourselves and enjoyed a pleasant discussion regarding music, life in the Keys, even Hurricane Irma. The lady turned out to be a very dear friend of the artist. I immediately knew that exchanging phone numbers would benefit the two of us, so I gave her my business card.

She held my card between her hands with appreciation, almost as if it was something of great value to her. I took the precaution of adding her name and number to my cell phone as well; her vibe had really struck me as extraordinary. As I began to type her first name into my device, she asked if I did not want to write her last name as well.

"Sure," I replied, and started typing the letters as she dictated them to me. As I finished, I looked at the screen in surprise. Her last name was very familiar!

Earlier that very morning I had looked at a Facebook page that I have just for acquaintances – one that I rarely use – and saw a memory that I had posted five years ago. It was a video of me playing the piano at a friend's place. Watching it that morning it occurred to me how long ago that was, and I wondered how that family was doing. I had not heard from them for years. Often times, for unknown reasons, lives take divergent paths. Now, here sitting next to me, was a daughter from that same family! I had never met her in person before. Now, had I been judgmental, had I not been open to walking over the bridge to see what was in her island, we would have never engaged in conversation, which was what led to our wonderful embrace upon meeting each other, which was overdue by at least five years.

HOW CAN DEATH HELP BUILD BRIDGES?

L et's have a look at yet another thought-provoking component of the Island Model: Death. In most cultures death is an absolute taboo. Don't get me wrong here, I am a positive thinker, and I love life! I am a realist, and I consider myself an idealist at the same time. Nevertheless, the fact is, I have not heard of any human who has made it out of the experience we call life alive. At the very moment of birth, we're already destined to die.

I consider life a gift. A gift to experience, explore, learn and grow, to love and live, and of course much more. When we meet people – other *islanders* – this can be a good thing, a challenge, or both at the same time. Challenges are great experiences for growth. We are usually curious when we meet new people. (Until we judge, prematurely on most occasions, anyway. I am not saying we cannot have our likes or dislikes. We all have the right to like certain things and not others, but judging goes beyond that). Our curiosity lasts exactly to that moment when we judge, have preexisting opinions, observe likes and dislikes, etc., and then act upon them. My personal take on this is that I doubt that we were born with the purpose of examining other humans to judge them and then try to change them; I believe this is conditioned.

Let's assume we go to a restaurant. Sitting at the table adjacent to ours is a handsome, young man. You may even think he appears intelligent as he carefully studies the menu and speaks knowledgeably to the waiter. Then the next thing you hear is a loud, but clear, burp. To your American sensibilities, suddenly the same man doesn't seem that polite anymore; you may rather think, "What a pig!" What changed? "What is, is," would be my first suggestion. When you first saw your table neighbor you projected an expectation based on his external appearance that would match the data you have collected in your life so far. Of course, this judgment depends on our own experiences and background. In many cultures, for example, burping indicates enjoyment of a meal and is completely acceptable. You access your personal, subjective data based on what you see, hear, feel. Then something happens that most of us humans are unaware of: we evaluate. We evaluate everything we perceive as either negative, positive, or neutral. Based on *how* we evaluate the perceived object or subject, we judge. Next, also without our conscious assistance, an avalanche of bio-chemicals make us *feel* uncomfortable or disgusted, or whatever else. And before we know it, a judgment is made and we condemn, in this case, the burper. As discussed earlier, that judgment will further the gap between our islands.

On another note: let us go back in time. Shortly after the above-mentioned young man was born, he was, just like you and I, encouraged to burp after breastfeeding/formula feeding, and parents or other caretakers applauded. When a baby cannot burp after a meal, parents are usually rather concerned. Would you agree? How confusing is this? When we are little we are encouraged to burp and when we grow up it is an unpleasant, even sinful act of shame?

When we are really annoyed by other peoples' behavior and/or actions we can use a relativity principle based on an idea by Carlos Castaneda (December 25. 1925 - April 27. 1998). Castaneda was an American author with a Ph.D. in anthropology whose 12 books have sold more than 28 million copies in 17 languages. He said: "Your death is always sitting on your shoulder, and you can ask any question." As death is a taboo subject in our society, many feel uncomfortable with this thought. Nevertheless, he suggests: "When you have really big problems next time, ask yourself if it really were as big, if you knew that you, at day X in time, let's say six months from now, weren't around." When you are afraid of this, you can use the small version of this relativity principle: When you're upset at a person, the burper, for example, ask yourself, how would you react if you knew that this *idiot* had only four weeks left of his life? Countless times I've seen that tolerance increases exponentially, because when related to death, this issue is suddenly, "Oh, no big deal!" Most likely this will lead directly to the relativity principle. Not the Einstein version of it, but one that helps us put situations in a different perspective. When you become aware of the fact and remind yourself that you're living in your island and others live in theirs, you already achieve a tremendous shift in your evolution as a mindful human being with an increased level of emotional intelligence.

THE FIXED STAR

A nother great tool to lessen argumentative encounters and build stronger bridges is to see the big picture. What is your goal? What is the long-term goal that you wish to achieve?

The term *fixed star* describes an extremely distant star whose position appears to be stationary. Nevertheless, *fixed stars* are not still-standing, not never-moving. They only appear to remain in constant position relative to other celestial bodies in our solar system from our earthly point of view. Realistically, fixed stars move at a very slow pace: by one degree in 72 years. I like to use this term as a metaphor in my one-on-one sessions, seminars, and workshops to visually describe the process of prioritizing when it comes to our goals. When you are clear regarding your goals, the first, most important step is already accomplished. (If you would like to discover a useful tool for *how* to find out what you really want, you can learn more in my book *The Formula for Finding True Love.)*

Life is consistently changing, and it is good to be rigid in some areas of our lives, yet flexible in others. If your goals are filled with integrity and authenticity, it could be worthwhile to make them a fixed star, metaphorically. When you turn those dream goals of yours into precious treasures so that it becomes easy to keep them in the front of your mind, you create your own fixed stars. Have a look at them in the big picture. Once you focus on your subjectively *special* goals, random obstacles on your journey towards achieving them become mere bumps in the road. Nothing more or less.

My beloved late uncle Hans Richter loved to sail. A little more than two decades ago he travelled to Mallorca, Spain to buy a sailboat. As soon as he laid eyes on the perfect vessel, Mariele, he put pen to paper and their union began. She was a pure beauty in my uncle's eyes. Of course, Hans wanted to try her capability on the waters as soon as they were officially together. He was ready to sail. The morning they left the marina, neither my uncle nor Mariele could know what awaited them. Hans sailed to the neighboring island Menorca, also geographically located in the Mediterranean Sea. Satisfied with each other, the new team, Hans and Mariele, followed their dream. Hans's first goal was to challenge the Gibraltar Strait, which is a narrow strait that connects the Mediterranean Sea to the Atlantic Ocean. This strait separates Gibraltar and Peninsular Spain in Europe from Morocco and Ceuta (Spain) in Africa. The adventure turned out to be greater than anticipated. As the nautical team approached the narrow part of the STROG (the nickname for the Strait of Gibraltar), the winds picked up unexpectedly. Hans navigated Mariele not only through the fierce gusts, but also safely into the Atlantic. From there, the next fixed star was the Canary Islands. Hans playfully handled Mariele through the rough Atlantic although she was built to be sailed by a crew, or so he said. Single-handedly, my uncle focused further west. As the currents were opportune that late summer in 1992, Hans decided to sail towards the center of the Atlantic Ocean to reach Cape Verde, which is officially the Republic of

Cabo Verde. (Genoese and Portuguese navigators discovered the islands around 1456).

Mariele

Repairs on the vessel were necessary, and Hans decided to wait out the season in Cape Verde to work patiently, yet effectively, on Mariele, all the while with his fixed star in mind. However, during a keen attempt to learn Portuguese, his goal, which had momentarily appeared stationary, altered once more. Now his focus was on the Amazon River. Crossing the Atlantic Ocean single-handedly became the fixed *star* for Hans. Nothing seemed impossible to him.

The previous spring he had attended a course to study celestial navigation in Munich, Germany. Phoenician sailors were quite accomplished navigators using primitive charts simply by observations of the sun and stars about 4,000 years ago (2000 B.C.E.); however, in the late twentieth century this caveman-like technique was still considered a contemporary skill, almost mandatory to courageous captains engaging in sailing journeys between continents. The sextant, an instrument that provided Mariners with a quite accurate means of determining the angle between the horizon, sun, moon, or stars, helped to determine latitude. With these ancient skills, my uncle embarked Mariele in São Vicente to reach for his fixed star, the Amazon River.

Shortly after entering the roughness of the most unpredictable – according to Hans – of all waters our globe possesses, the boat's generator broke in the middle of nowhere. Food supplies diminished quickly. Fishing for plenty of fish was an option, but not to the gentleness of Hans's soul. When catching an edible creature, my uncle stared into its eyes and dropped it right back into freedom, feeling disgusted at the thought of killing it and then eating it. Starving became his new diet.

Navigating by the natural objects located outside of Earth's atmosphere was the only presumable way to find Brazil. When the winds picked up in the middle of one stormy night Hans was forced to reef the sails and lower his storm anchor. Carefully, he crawled out of the cabin. All of a sudden, the boom greeted him roughly and broke his ribs.

Hans could barely move but he would not let go of his fixed star, the Amazon River. Nights and days of sailing through storms challenged him to keep his focus. Ultimately, his near-death experiences at sea dissipated once he entered the basin of the largest river in South America, the Amazon. Mariele and Hans made it safely through rough salty waters, sleepless nights, starvation, celestial navigation, injuries, and later, a rendezvous with penguins in the southernmost continent. What literally kept him afloat towards Brazil was this one single thought he would never lose sight of: his fixed star!

In total, he eventually crossed the Atlantic Ocean five times single-handedly. One of these journeys earned him and Mariele the prestigious Trans Ocean Prize for sailing 22,000 nautical miles single-handedly over a period of 402 days. The prize was delivered to him in Hamburg, Germany. His initial fixed star of crossing the Gibraltar Strait had evolved into so much more: having one goal only propelled him towards others.

Preisträger

Preis	**TO-Preis 1993**
Preisträger	**Hans Richter**
Yacht (Typ)	**Mariele** (Standfast 47)
Entfernung	**22000 NM**
Dauer	**402 Tage**

Reisebeschreibung
Einhand von Europa in den Südatlantik und Südpazifik um Kap Hoorn und zurück ins Mittelmeer

Evidently my uncle's adventures are sincerely special to me, personally. They also have huge educational value, considering the above-mentioned fixed star metaphor. Next time you think about engaging in arguments for known or unknown reasons, remember your true goal(s). Whether they be personal, regional, national, international, global, universal, traditional, cultural, etc. – what is your goal? What is it that you really want to achieve? Priorities never lie! Not in business, not in personal affairs, neither nationally nor globally, financially nor ethically, nor morally. Is it you, or are society's expectations driving you? Do you hold on to traditional habits without scrutinizing their validity? How many of your beliefs are no longer supportive of your personal growth?

I know of a German cattleman called Volker who inherited a farm in the Allgäu area (Southern Swabia) from his father, who inherited the ranch from his grandfather. The family was known for their dairy cow breed. Nevertheless, farming had changed over the decades and generations. To keep the family business running and financially secure, Volker had to come up with a miracle to increase their milk production. The only car wash in the village had closed down when its owner died. None of the owner's descendants wanted to manage the business, so they listed it for sale. Volker had a brilliant idea: he could use the car wash plant for his farm. He bought the equipment and emptied one third of his stable. Covering the ground with straw, he then randomly installed the rotating brushes. He directed the cattle into their new free-range. Other farmers in the village made fun of Volker's curiosity. They shook their heads in disbelief. Nonetheless, the cows enjoyed their newly-gained freedom. They curiously inspected the colorful rotating brushes. The animals soon found pleasure in leaning and rubbing themselves against the fancy car-wash-massage. Not only were their coats the shiniest, the boosted circulation increased their milk production as well, much to Volker's delight.

He later also installed a sound system that played Mozart to his cows! A German television crew made a documentary about this contemporary, out-of-the-box cattle farm. Volker followed his fixed star: his goal was to flourish in business. He was rather courageous in trying something no one had done before. He kept the values from the old family tradition that supported his goal and eliminated those that didn't make sense any longer. He made space for the new, tried out ideas, and continued to experiment, to improve himself and the farm.

Culturally we often are caught up in centuries-old manners. Society is rarely supportive of change. Most humans are afraid of the unknown, the unfamiliar, and prefer to keep things as they are, and supposedly always were. However, evolution is unstoppable. Consider our cells. Billions of them die every single day, and at the same time, new ones are born. That's natural rejuvenation. I think this process is necessary for *homo sapiens*, not just physically, but in fact mentally and psychologically as well.

The fear of being different and therefore not accepted, likable, and/or lovable, often keeps us humans trapped. Trapped in our island, trapped in false beliefs that may have expired, trapped in expectations: these all lead to dependence. For example, if Susie is in a good mood she compliments me. That feels good. If

Susie is in a bad mood, she ignores me, and that makes me sad. Can you see the dependence here? When we are doing the best we can, acting and behaving with integrity, what Susie says or does, or doesn't say or doesn't do, becomes less important. We have the right to make mistakes. Think of Edison: how often did he fail while inventing the light bulb? He made 1,000 unsuccessful attempts! We have the right to make mistakes, too. Once we are aware of our greater goal(s) – our fixed star(s) – mistakes turn out to be little nothings in the big picture.

It takes self-confidence to accept the consequences when we stand out from the norm. What is the norm? Who rules over social expectations? What is 'normal' anyway? Normality is usually considered to be the opposite of being deviant, eccentric, or unusual. Nevertheless, definitions regarding normality vary between people, eras, places, times, cultures, situations, etc.

In 1914, when my German grandmother was born, the norm in Prussia was not to share any public display of affection. Growing up seven decades later, I remember seeing my grandparents holding hands and even sharing a kiss once in a while. Nowadays, we can see couples kissing publicly wherever we look, and no one seems to feel offended. Norms shift along with changing societal standards. The challenge I see today lies more in civilizational shock. Cultures are mingled and mixed more than ever before in history. We judge more openly than anyone dared in the past. Everything that diverges from the norm is automatically perceived as a threat; and threats have an immediate impact on our brain stem, the reptilian brain. Our fight, flight, or freeze program runs automatically without any conscious effort, which increases the levels of cortisol and adrenaline in our system. Not only does this neuro-biological avalanche affect our immune system in an instant, it also influences our behavior. Nevertheless, behavior is always a choice. Once we choose integrity over traditions, love over judgment, respect over selfishness and the need to be right, we may even reach a level of peaceful thinking, thoughtfulness, consideration, acceptance, and tolerance beyond what we humans as a species have encountered in life so far. This helps us tremendously in our attempt to build bridges, and bridge natural and artificial gaps.

In my seminars, workshops, one-on-one, and group sessions I teach what I live by: "Say what you mean, and mean what you say."

As if it were that simple! I don't know of a single culture where saying what we mean and meaning what we say would be standard, and where the upcoming generation is taught to live by this creed. Nevertheless, our communication and behavior become clearer to other islanders when we stand for what we think, speak, and do, and when these three are in alignment.

FROM CONDITIONING TO INTEGRITY

We are all conditioned (or brainwashed, rather) to a certain degree: some more than others. Don't get offended, dear reader; I include myself in this equation. The question to challenge now is: "How can we un-condition ourselves?" The prestigious Harvard Business School acknowledges integrity as one key element to success, and promotes their slogan, "Engage with ideas to make you a better leader." HBS professor Michael C. Jensen states in an interview that appeared in *The Magazine of the Rotman School of Management*: "An individual is whole and complete when their word is whole and complete, and their word is whole and complete when they honor their word."

I couldn't agree more. Let's go back to the roots and observe closely *whom* we were born as. When we arrived into this world, we looked curiously around to explore and learn. What our caretakers believed, said, and did, developed into standard(s) for us. Language, religion, and tradition were forced on us as children. However, I wish to inspire you, dear reader, to rethink, rediscover, re-challenge, and remember/re-member (more about that later). My wish for you is to be the kind, loving, creative, caring human you were born to be, and not the fearful, angry, sad, reactive, etc. person you became. Be the successful leader in your own life. Jensen and his co-authors describe integrity as a purely positive phenomenon that has nothing to do with the polar *good vs. bad* or *wrong vs. right* behaviors. As a comparison, they refer to gravity: "If you violate the law of integrity as we define it, you get hurt just as if you try to violate the law of gravity with no safety device[1]. I personally have high hopes that, now that HBS publishes and teaches the personal and organizational benefits of honoring one's word, they will be widely heard, and the appreciation of integrity overall may grow globally. Imagine if we lived in a world where we could trust a person when they stated, "I will call you tomorrow," or, "I'll take care of it right now, and get back to you," or a more consequential statement in the early days of a relationship: "I am single and I want an exclusive, committed, monogamous relationship with you."

---

1 Jensen, Michael C. "Integrity: Without it Nothing Works." Harvard Business School Working Paper, No. 10-042, November 2009.

I know of a mother who was rather upset with her teenage son. He got caught lying several times and Mrs. Miller called him to have a talk. She lounged on her canapé (sofa), her son standing before her. As she reprimanded him for lying, the doorbell rang, interrupting her. The mother said, "Tell them I am not here." The son walked over to the entrance, opened the door, and did as his mother said, then walked back to Mommy as she continued: "Next time I catch you lying, you'll be grounded for two weeks." Bang! There it was! Here, another example: A father rants at his son for not being respectful towards women, but makes comments like this within earshot of his son: "Hey, do you guys remember that bachelor's party in that little strip joint? Those stupid [insert sexist profanity] talking about falling in love?" and laughs out loud. (These are true stories.)

Double standards don't work well, especially in the long-term. Even Hollywood is awakening slowly from its Sleeping Beauty nap. More and more men and women are speaking out about their experiences of harassment and abuse. Hollywood is about to change into a better and hopefully fairer platform for actors and all those working in the industry. And it is about time, I'd say, that we evolve into a society where equality and respect is on the menu of all daily agendas, not only in Hollywood.

"Be the change that you wish to see in the world."

– Mahatma Gandhi

How can we possibly successfully continue to expect specific attitudes and forms of behavior when we ourselves practice the opposite? Soccer is a ballgame that is played globally. The rules are the same, no matter where the players compete. In 2014, Brazil hosted the World Cup and the rules of the game were clear. In 2018, Russia will be the organizer of the same World Cup and the rules will not have changed. Imagine a team disregarding the FIFA rules? Disqualification would be the eventual outcome. Simple as that. So why do some individuals feel authorized to play unfairly while expecting others to obey the rules? Why is it that in sports, regulations are clear and violations have immediate consequences, while in other areas of life, things are much murkier?

When two islanders interact with one another, it is necessary, and healthy, to openly agree to rules, set clear boundaries, and make transparent agreements. No one island is more precious than any other; they are simply different.

Diverse contents and contexts make islands and their residents unique. I have the right to disagree with the angry mother who reprimands lying while being a liar herself and indirectly teaching her son that lying is okay. I can also dislike the disrespectful father who teaches his son *how* to continue behaving disrespectfully towards women in general, while hypocritically preaching respect for women. The one way – the only way – I see to establish and live a content life is to make clear agreements and set boundaries that both parties respect equally. When one party decides and/or chooses to disrespect the acknowledged agreements, their behavior obviously shows that they do not want to participate in the common interaction. This might be a hurtful experience. Nevertheless, I question why would you want to play with someone – actually, *anyone* – who clearly shows that they do not want to play with you? Only when the guidelines are set in stone, as they say, discussed in the open, and agreed upon, can we expect to be on the same page. That is when joint ventures are fun, grow into fulfillment, and may develop into absolute happiness.

OBSERVATION COMES FIRST – FOLLOWED BY INTERPRETATION

A few months ago, while residing in South Florida, I heard a hurricane warning that had to be taken seriously. I had lived in South Beach, the southernmost part of the (in)famous Miami Beach, for eight years. Societies change over time, and I felt the time was just about right to move on to another place, to find a new home. My personal life was almost fairytale-like and the stage was set for the grand finale. I had met my knight in shining armor – he was charming, too! – nearly three years prior. Long story short, I ended up in Marathon, which is located in the Florida Keys (Middle Keys). What a lovely, precious spot on this planet. Paradisiac.

Artistic. The perfect place for writing and serving my clients. As most of my sessions are conducted over Skype or WebEx, I can work from anywhere. There had been warnings of tropical storms and hurricanes in the past; luckily I had not yet been introduced to the harm and anger nature occasionally presents.

But Irma was on her way, stronger and larger than anticipated, heading towards my beloved Florida Keys. *Veni, vidi, vici.* She came, she saw, and she thought she conquered us with her violent landfall in my chosen paradise. The mandatory evacuation announced by Monroe County forced me, along with thousands of my fellow islanders, to leave the Florida Keys. Like most of my neighbors, I had prepared my home with plywood to protect windows and doors, shifted all possible flying objects from outdoors to indoors, and evacuated for good. Until the very last minute, my hopes were high that Irma would change her path and leave us undisturbed.

The days that followed changed our future and rewrote the history of the area. Thousands of families left their homes and fled further north, to what they thought was safety. Unpredictably, Irma changed direction and chased thousands up through the state of Florida, even other states. I was incredibly lucky to have had shelter in Miami. The storm hit, and the nerve-wracking waiting began. When will we be able to go back? When will they allow us into the Keys? Days went by without electricity, television, or Internet connectivity. On day six, residents southwest of Mile Marker 85 were finally allowed access, with either proof of residency or a sticker on the dashboard, to drive into the

Keys and discover the magnitude of the impact Irma had caused.

Never before in my life have I seen destruction to such an extent. The familiar green color of the flora had disappeared, burnt by the speedy winds and sea salt. Homes were simply gone; favorite spots disappeared into nothingness. I couldn't recognize most of the areas as I drove towards my home. Luckily, my lovely friends and my spouse were with me when my driveway came into sight. As we approached the unrecognizable neighborhood, I still had high hopes that the 60-year-old house may have survived just fine. Our front porch is four steps above ground level, which is almost equal to sea level. In the past 60 years, there had never been a flood that reached higher than the first step of our front porch.

As the vegetation had suffered tremendous damage, access to the driveway was quite difficult. I wanted to walk into the yard and see that the house was dry and my tangible belongings had survived just fine. I stepped out of the car, wearing construction boots for protection, and gradually made my way along the driveway towards my little house. I had to climb over debris up to my thighs, fallen palm trees, and knee-high sand. Finally, I reached the porch. I reminisced the thousand times I had walked towards this entrance to step into my little sanctuary.

However, this time was different. The stench that hit my nose filled me with disgust. Grassy Key had its name for a reason: depending on the seasonal winds and currents, plenty of sea grass washed onshore at the end of the property. This time it wasn't just the decomposing sea grass that I could smell. There was also the stench of dead Iguanas, leftovers from freezers, and I cannot fathom or describe what else. I headed towards the entrance, still clinging to hope, but what I saw was not comparable to anything to which I had a point of reference. The ocean had been so powerful that it had burst the floor wide open, apparently surging into the living room first, and then all over the house. As the water receded, the hole in the floor had been large enough to take most of my material belongings. Things simply disappeared, never to be found again.

The damage was factual. Its interpretation was up to me. Remember: focus on what you can control/change; stop focusing on what you cannot control/change. I acknowledged the loss. It hurt a lot. I also realized that no one can take away what I have within me – my heart and my brains! So I decided to share what I had left and started free group meetings for the Florida Keys Irma survivors to handle stress and PTSD in ways that rather empower instead of drain us. Magically, within a week, all was organized, and a small, but very precious group that was open to explore and experience empowering thinking processes came together. The gratitude I've experienced in this particular group is extremely dear to me. Is the cleanup a mess and hassle? Oh, it surely is. Can I change it? No. Still, I was fully responsible for my interpretation of the event.

Remember, we are all given the gift of choice. We can always choose to take a moment before we interpret; in other words, judge, evaluate, give meaning. Everyone has the right to judge, and the more we evolve into emotionally intelligent beings, we can take responsibility for our judgments before even developing them. Becoming aware of the process, how judgment develops – not only in us, but in others too – helps us increase understanding, tolerance, and acceptance. Building bridges and looking at our islands and others' creates closeness instead of distance. They also have the gift of choice, just as we do. Other *islanders* are conditioned; so are we. We have more in common than we sometimes like to admit.

REMEMBER; RE-MEMBER

I invite you to have a look at the word *remember* for a moment, from a different perspective. To me, *re-* is an indication to do something again, in a different, hopefully better way: rethink, rebuild, reestablish, refurbish, reinforce, etc. My strong belief that no one is born racist can be used as an example here. The interpretation of, and reaction to the amount of pigment in the skin is individually up to each of us. A pigment count is genetically indicated. Wouldn't you agree? As the observer of that factual count, we then evaluate what we perceive as either negative, positive, or neutral. This evaluation process happens quickly and subconsciously. Once evaluated, we interpret our perception. Judgment is about to happen. Nonetheless, it is possible to remember what we can control. Skin pigmentation is out of our control. I wish to inspire you to focus on what you *can* control. Remember, we humans are conditioned. We all live in our own little world, our unique island.

Remember, and re-member to become (again) who you were born to be. I also wish for you to become a member of a new society, to become the leader of your own life, and live a leaders' life in exemplary ways. I hope that you will inspire, and re-wire your brain, which is an immeasurably powerful instrument, greater than any computer on earth, thus far. Building bridges can lead to great results and success. Everything you read, hear, watch, listen to, and do, has an impact – direct or indirect – on you. I wish for you to choose wisely and take inventory from time to time, as it can be very helpful. Please, use it.

I recall a conversation I had with my friend Joanna. She narrated a time in her life when she was single and wanted to meet her Mr. Right. She traveled quite frequently. One day, waiting at a gate at the airport, she literally bumped into another passenger. They engaged in friendly small talk. To her surprise, boarding the plane, her seat was reserved next to the person she had bumped into earlier. They continued to exchange their ideas about life, their dreams, and how to gain the knowledge and skills to achieve them. She openly admitted that she would love to fall in love again after having lost her husband in the previous year. The passenger next to her got rather excited, and explained a foolproof way to find a perfect partner. Joanna got just as excited. She was willing to try whatever it would take. The passenger asked her to write a list – very detailed – describing all of the characteristics, character traits, habits, routines, hobbies, strengths, style, behavior, preferences, etc. that she wanted in the perfect partner. Joanna started her list, trying to catalogue all she was aiming to find in her future spouse. After a second cup of green tea, Joanna proudly presented her lengthy script to her wise seatmate, who carefully studied it. Then came the eagerly anticipated response: "This is a great list, Joanna. All you listed is fabulous. *This is exactly who you need to become.* The person described in your list will fall head-over-heels in love with you, and he will never let you go!"

Joanna found her spouse a couple of months later, got engaged six months after her first date, and moved to Florida to live with her future husband. She described her dream partner profoundly at 32,000 feet cruising altitude. She became aware that she wanted to become the person with all the characteristics, character traits, habits, etc. that she had listed. She focused on what was in her control – her personal growth – and in doing so found her perfect partner.

Not long ago, a young woman called me to complain about her spouse's name-calling. She was clearly upset. During our conversation, it became clear to me that her attitude and choice of words was similar to what she was upset and complaining about. I believe everyone has the right to complain. In some outdated businesses, leaders still believe that "the customer is always right." I disagree. Attitude matters, updated communication skills are needed, respect should be taught, offers, services, and job descriptions should be defined and clarified. This is what I believe will support businesses to survive, flourish, evolve, and succeed. The above-mentioned woman can become someone who communicates healthily and appropriately. Once she puts forth an effort to choose her words wisely and respectfully, which undoubtedly requires self-discipline and other skills, her quest for respectful and polite conversation in her relationship will have the grounds to become standard.

I cannot mention often enough that change needs to happen in your own island first before you can inspire changes outside your territory. Albert Einstein verbalized a thought I'd like to share with you: "Everybody is a genius. But if you judge a fish by its ability to climb a tree it will live its whole life believing that it is stupid." You are a genius, and so are others. Building bridges instead of burning them brings us closer, brings cultures together, and makes life on Earth an amazing adventure. I wish you much joy in discovering new shores.

AFTERWORD

"To gain access to new shores you have to leave the old one first."

– My Grandmother Kobe

As I sit in North Miami Beach this very evening of the 16th of December, 2017, at a favorite spot of mine, I wonder about the magnitude of impact my words may have on you. Be assured, that it is not my purpose to change you, dear reader. What you do with the information written here is out of my control. So, instead I focus on what I can control, and in this particular case, it is the words I am writing. Life is a never-ending learning experience. We have our individual ideas about how we would like to live our lives. After living as a house guest for the past three months, as my home was severely damaged by Hurricane Irma, and is still not habitable to this day, I realize a little more every day. I have new insight as to what I would like to experience more in my life, and what I want to experience less; or, more precisely, what I want no part of in my life. Visiting other islands, and maybe one day even yours, dear reader, is my wish. I want to see laughter and even tears, commitment and empathy, integrity, love and hugs, and so much more. I want to experience more of all the good life provides. More fun, more intimacy, more loving words, more understanding, more harmony, and less humiliation, dishonesty, and cruelty. I wish the same for you. You are the one who is responsible for what you change or continue to experience. Sound unrealistic? Well, let me put it this way: If your pattern is to stay where you are not appreciated – may this be emotionally, mentally, physically, or otherwise – look at your pattern and find out what the root of your behavior is. Not theirs, whoever they are. They are responsible for their actions. Does Karma exist? I cannot prove it, and I honestly don't know. Nevertheless, you can always choose how you behave, respond, and react. With or without Karma, your choices will have consequences. We can't predict when the last grain of sand in our life will slip through the hourglass. I encourage you to take full responsibility for your island, its content, beliefs, habits, etc. Take an inventory at times, keep what supports you, and let go of all that will hold you back from living the best life you can possibly live.

TESTIMONIALS

A couple of weeks after the devastating Hurricane Irma came through our beautiful Florida Keys, I was feeling pretty lost, down, and in despair. Someone posted on Facebook a group meeting to help the citizens of Marathon deal with the feelings of grief that were all around us. From our first meeting on, I was looking forward to every Thursday group meeting. Daisy has shown to us her commitment, dedication, and expertise to help us understand why we have all the feelings we are experiencing. Once I discovered the Island idea through her teachings, I was set free of many of my crazy emotions, and for that I am in many ways so grateful.

– Lily Leitner

*W*hen I came to Daisy I thought I already had a good understanding of psychology and relationships – that was until she started cracking open my mind and revealed some truly invaluable new concepts for me to build on. Her Island Model taught me about personal responsibility, and how to free myself from taking responsibility for others in such a simple and succinct way that I was shocked I had never looked at it that way before. It truly is liberating to view the world in this way from both an intra-personal and interpersonal perspective. Thank you, Daisy, for all your amazing concepts and ideas that have radically changed the way I view myself and the world!

– Zak Pinder

OTHER BOOKS BY THE AUTHOR

✧ *5+2 = **The Formula for Finding True Love***

Kindle:
https://www.amazon.com/Formula-Finding-True-Love-ebook/dp/B0719SXXNH

Paperback:
https://www.amazon.com/Formula-Finding-True-Love/dp/1546973605/ref=tmm_pap_swatch_0?_encoding=UTF8&qid=&sr=

✧ ***One Nail at A Time*** *– Autobiography (coming soon)*
✧ ***Blook*** *– A Blog-Book (coming soon)*

THANK YOU

I want to give heartfelt thanks to all human beings who have crossed my path and my island, and have invited me to theirs. I learned from all of you, and your islands.

Special thanks to my editors and those who read my manuscript in the early stages. Beth Dorsey and Sarah Chalmers, thank you very much for your final polishing and suggestions.

Thank you, Carlos Scandiffio, for the illustrations.

I am extremely grateful for my teachers: Vera F. Birkenbihl, Dr. Elvira Babindak, Dr. Gyula Biro, Richard Bandler, Robert Smith, Gary Craig, Dawson Church, Eric Dickhaus, Prof.

Dr. Gerald Huether, Ed Gibbson, John Earhart, Zsuzsanna Papai, and many more.

My son, thank you for reminding me that your island is not mine, and your journey is all yours.

My dear friends are my chosen family. I am grateful to have a few real friends all over the globe.

Thank you, dear clients. You share so much insight with me and give me the opportunity to learn from you while observing you making healthy changes in your lives and relationships. Your feedback regarding the Island Model inspired me to write it down in the form of this book. Lily Leitner, you gave me the "kick" I appreciate so much, that led me to finally sit down and write.

I am grateful for the gift of my life, the gift of all the life surrounding me, and the gift of choice. I learn and grow every single day to become the best I can possibly be.

My heart is always with my parents, my beloved brother, and uncle Hans. You gave me the foundation and values, education and possibilities that helped me become who I am today. I feel privileged to have had you in my life, even though it was only for a limited time.